FROM BLACK SHEEP TO GOD'S CHOSEN ONE

ANNE BLACK

Published by BooxAi
ISBN: 979-8-89383-004-0

I dedicate this book to my Lord and Savior Jesus Christ and wonderful children and grandchildren.

"Rejoice in the Lord always. Again I will say, rejoice."

Philippians 4:4

ONE

Growing Up

I was born on August 29th, 1967 on my mother's birthday at noon, "the hottest part of the day", as my mother would put it. She was a narcissist. My dad was an empath. He was a quiet, peaceful individual. Praise God. I needed it. I would not have made it without my dad's unconditional love.

Growing up I felt and looked different from my other six siblings. My mother had seven children, three of which are my dad's. I, now, know it was those other gentlemen that made her a narcissist. At four years old the Lord Jesus save me. I knew them I was to love and serve the Lord.

At ten years old, I got in a terrible car accident. I broke every bone in my body. It took me about a month to go back to school. It's just by the Grace of God that I am here.

Right about that time I got a mouth on me I would tell my family if they were not doing Right. I had my intuition, even, back then. My mother thought I was a smart lick. She let me know she was not having me talk back. She beat me mercilessly.

My pointing out the truth didn't t, seem to bother anyone, but my mother hated the truth. Narcissist hates God and God's people. They are the devil's minions. They love telling lies, and putting curses and spells on people.

My mother was a stay-at-home mom. She was exceptional at that. She kept us fed and imma u late at all times. She's usually nice until she gets into her Narcissistic rage. I got the worst of it. It got worse as she got older. On her deathbed, she was telling lies.

"And we know that all things work together for good to those who love God, to those who are the called according to His purpose."

Romans 8:28

TWO

Call a Spade, a Spade

I didn't t make it easy, for my mother to love me. I called a Spade, a Spade. If something was wrong. I called it out. I believe the Lord was using my mouthpiece to change her. Half the things I said. I didn't t understand. The Lord was calling her out and she wasn't t having that. So, of course, she ends up hating me for it.

I tried many times to quit speaking. God would always win. I keep speaking out. I thought it would help her. She didn't t want to hear the truth from me. I love my mother. Still do. I felt compassion for her as a child.

I believe she saw my life purpose and didn't want me to serve the Lord. God will not allow anyone to steal your life purpose. I believe as a mother, my job is to encourage my children to pursue God's purpose in their life. I felt at times like Joseph and his evil brothers.

I knew right it's just no one wants to hear of it.

Growing up, it wasn't t all bad. I got along well with my siblings, even my oldest sister, Melva.

We siblings had many fun times. We'd play with our dolls, or dishes or play baseball. That was my favorite pass time.

"For the wages of sin is death, but the gift of God is eternal life in Christ Jesus our Lord."

Romans 6:23

THREE

Teenage Years

As I got into my teens, needless to say, I got bolder calling out the truth. My mother grew to despise me. She ignores me for days. Even if I spoke to her. She'd say things like dog eat your supper. I didn't t know what it meant, but I knew it wasn't good.

She'd sometimes call me a dog. I am my mother's daughter. I wouldn't back down either. I do it for good I am not a mean-spirited person, but I'm also not afraid to speak the truth. I

hates injustices.

After my older sisters left home. It was just my sister, Rose, and myself, left with my mother.

When she gets in her rage. She'd tell my sister to tell that dog to do this or that. Referring to me. I felt like Cinderella. I get to do all the work and get treated badly.

There were days when I asked the Lord to take me home. It was horrible. The Lord would let me know. I will be fine. He never left my side. He made me stronger, both, physically and mentally.

Remember, beloved, that which does not kill you, makes you strong.

"For by grace you have been saved through faith, and that not of yourselves; it is the gift of God, not of works, lest anyone should boast."

Ephesians 2:8-9

FOUR

Marriage

At 22 years old. I met the man of my dreams. My husband. A blond hair and blue-eyed beauty. I didn't t know it at the time. He was a Narcissist. I went from the frying pan, straight into the fire.

He was amazingly nice at first. There were signs he was mad at God. I guess I didn't t want to see it. Love is blind.

Huge mistake. Anyone you put ahead of God is an idol. It won't work. God will not play second fiddle to anyone, beloved. The Lord was always with me. I was not supposed to do Him like this. I would apologize and he'd forgive. It was a cycle.

Three years into our marriage was fairly well. Then I had my daughter, Ashley, The pressure of parenthood. It brought out his narcissistic nature. In rage. I decided to raise my kids on my own. I had to divorce him mentally. To keep my sanity. Three years later. I had my son, Emmanuel. It means God is with us. The Lord let me know he is His intangible presence in my life. God is good.

I praise God, for my children. What a wonderful gift. They have brought such delight into my life. Such Peace and gratefulness. My dreams came through, to serve God and be a mother.

In my marriage, my husband wasn't always hateful. That's how narcissists do. They are the devil's minions. They love-bomb you to gain your love and trust. Then they stab you in the back, ignore, you, hold intimacy from you, and cause fights.

I left him twice. He came back twice. He thought marriages were forever. It is.

There is no I in a marriage. It's we. He wanted me to do unlawful things with him. I wouldn't. I stood my ground. As Christians, we have to stand against anyone and say, No. sir, I will not do it.

I love my husband, but you can't live with everyone you love. The Jesus factor, won't allow it. You'll have to divorce them, mentally. To survive. I had my children to raise.

And like adding insult to injury. My sister, Melva, was letting me feel my marriage was bad, I wasn't t a good mother. I didn't tell her about my marriage, I didn't t think I was poor. God bless me with amazing children and grandchildren.

That's another thing narcissist do, they project their life on you.

She's about keeping up with the Joneses. Working hard, adults pleasure and partying. She didn't like children. I couldn't have her with mine. Children are smart. They sensed her.

It's sad. But we had nothing in common. I was about the family she was about fun. She said many times she's bored. I'd tell her to join a church. We live in different states.

I would have loved to have a sister to tell my troubles to, but it didn't happen that way. I got better. I got Jesus. When you have the best, you don t want the rest. My husband used to say, you don't go out for hamburgers when you have steak at home.

Today I don't have either of them in my life. I am most happy. I want to enjoy, whatever little time I have here on earth. I forgave both and wish them well, just not with me.

God bless me with a wonderful life. Praise God.

"As it is written: 'There is none righteous, no, not one.'"

Romans 3:10

FIVE

Prison Ministry

My husband did construction. He doesn't always do right. His motto was it for that. Whatever they do to me, I'll do to them. I told him that was the wrong way to look at life. He wouldn't listen.

Anyway, he didn't t finish a job he contracted for. He went to prison for fraud.

It was the hardest time for me, I didn't t have anyone to help, not even family. I was alone.

Not quite. I had the Only Person. Who has always been there for me? At all times, JESUS

See I love the Lord, but was using Him.

I am not proud of it. I brought this on myself. You could love the Lord and at the same time be mad at Him, or using Him. As it was my case. One day, the Lord will tell you to stop. A stubborn mind makes a soft behind. I mean the Lord say me down, on the floor.

I was 38 years old. That day I came back to be with

my daddy and my Lord. It was the hardest of times, and the best of times. I finally had peace.

I praise God. That God used my husband to teach me a lesson. I praise God, that He didn't use my children. He wanted me to be happy. My husband put himself in prison. God used it to bring me back to Him, where I belong with my Father and King Jesus.

After my husband got out of prison. The Lord bless me with a men's Prison Ministry.

Amazing. It was the best 10 years of my life.

Out of our mess, beloved, God will give us a message. I live my life every day. Romans 8 28. That says, For we know that all things work together for good, to those who are called according to His purpose.

Today nothing phases me. God is in control. The world better knows that. He is not going to allow these devil folks to mistreat His children. They are about to be sat down, on the floor.

Although beloved, we have these devil folks around. Praise God, we also have the sweet Holy Spirit, inside us, that we don't t have to be like them. We are not Karen's. Our Father keeps us 50 steps ahead. I believe if you are not Jesus. I don t need to explain myself to you. I believe 2024 is the year to pull out our sword for the injustices in our lives. I saying no more. It stops here.

"Yea, though I walk through the valley of the shadow of death, I will fear no evil; For You are with me."

Psalm 23:4

SIX

Out of Body Experience

I had a Body Experience, that brought about this book. On Friday, November 7th. At about 11 pm. I had a death spell put on my life. I was asleep. I felt like my heart and lungs were being ripped out of my body. I had a fever and chills. I couldn't t breathe. I had to open my mouth to breathe. It felt like my arms were being ripped out of its socket. It was excruciating. I was asking the Lord if I was going to die. He said Yes.

I knew it was spiritual warfare. I knew I had to fight for my life. I put my arm straight in the

Air. I'm in fighting mode. I start shouting Jesus, Jesus, Jesus. I started praying for all the saints

I can remember

To pray for me.

I was exhausted and fell asleep. It was then I felt my spiritual body left my earthly body. I hover over my body.

In the corner of the room, I saw a big black bird-like creature looking up at me. Very sinister.

It looks like it wanted to pounce on the sleeping body.

At this point, the Lord turns on the light. I saw it. And again I started screaming Jesus, Jesus, Jesus.

The creature went through the wall. It disappeared. I fell asleep. I was exhausted. I woke up Saturday, and my arms felt out of joint. I asked the Lord, What happened last night? He told me someone put a death spell on me. He brought me back to life. His Chosen.

No amount of spells will stop his purpose in life. I ask the Lord to get these devil folks out of my life. I am tired of them.

My beloved, No weapons form against God's children will prosper. If folks don't put their trust in the Lord Jesus Christ, to save them. They are going to hell. Hell was made for the devil and his angels, not for humans.

Be smart and do the right thing. Ask Jesus to save you, **TODAY**.

To my beloved and Saints out there I love you all. Amen.

About the Author

I'm Ann Black, and I reside in the vibrant city of Dallas, Texas, alongside my cherished family. My life is devoted to serving God, whether it be within the walls of my church, in the heart of our community, or wherever the divine guidance of the Lord beckons me.

One could say that my dream is as vast as the Texas sky, for I yearn to illuminate the path to salvation for all souls, to guide them towards embracing the grace of our Savior. Indeed, the promise of the Lord's imminent return fills me with boundless anticipation. For on that glorious day, He shall descend from the heavens, gathering His beloved children to dwell in eternal splendor. Oh, what a magnificent and joyous occasion that shall be!

With unwavering faith and fervent hope, I eagerly await the fulfillment of this divine promise, and I strive each day to spread His light and love to all who cross my path.

Come quickly, Lord Jesus.

Blessings,

Anne Black